The Biggest Problem in the World

The Biggest Problem in the World

*Our Problem with Problems
and Why Truth Matters*

Ronald Balzan

A CIP catalogue record for this book is available from the British Library.

ISBN 978 1 8383716 0 9

For us, who suffer unnecessarily

Contents

Acknowledgments

Very little in life is done alone, despite what we sometimes tell ourselves, and this handbook is no exception. Don't let its length fool you—this little book was a decade or more in the making, although most of that time was dedicated to study, research and thought. The actual writing took about a year. In 1657, the French philosopher and mathematician Blaise Pascal wrote (in French, of course), "I have made this [letter] longer than usual because I have not had time to make it shorter." I did the opposite: I took the time to make this book shorter.

A number of people have been by my side as this work unfolded, but no one more so than my partner, Brian McCarter. I had questions that nobody had answered, so I began searching for the answers myself. I didn't know where my research was going to take me, and there was no guarantee that it was going to take me anywhere—I simply let the facts guide me. And through the challenges, the ups and downs, Brian has been by my side, supporting me in so many ways. I cannot thank him enough, and I'm fortunate to have met him.

I'd also like to thank my parents, Ron and Kathy; my sister, Shannon, who left us too early; my grandmother Arlene, who was born before her time; and my stepmother, Mary. Much of whom I've become is because of them.

In addition to Brian, there are the friends who took an interest in my work, encouraged me and inspired me to press on, each in their own wonderful ways: J. Whitney Stevens, Bridget McCarthy, Grace Garinger, Harry Fox Davies, Josh Spector, Lee Gottsegen, Steve Hammer, David Peterson, Lisa

Vehrenkamp, Barbara LaVallee, Aleksandr Vishnevskiy, Judith Lindsay, Rebecca Fogg, Cynthia Hayes and others. They asked questions, listened to me, reviewed drafts and cared. Some also travelled to Edinburgh to see my shows at the Fringe.

Ah, the Fringe! In 2018 and 2019, wanting to start sharing this work with the general public and trying to figure out how best to do so, I wrote and performed a show at the Edinburgh Fringe. I had never done anything like it, but John-David Henshaw and Annie Marrs, of Sweet Venues, took a chance and gave me a stage. First it was terrifying, then it was thrilling, and I was hooked! The shows were well attended, and I loved interacting with the interested audiences. I also learned a lot about how to talk about my work to a wide audience. Thank you, JD, Annie, James and all of the others at Sweet and the Fringe as well as everyone who attended my shows there and in New York.

Of course, I wouldn't have had this handbook to write or a show to give if it weren't for the work that led me to answers to some of my questions. And I'm not sure I would have continued searching for them without the support of my supervisors, route coordinator and assessors in the Faculty of Education at Cambridge, perhaps in ways of which they are not aware: Professor Christine Howe, Michelle Ellefson, Sara Baker, Ros McLellan and Julia Flutter. They challenged me in my research, helped me to better organize and express my thoughts and findings, and by taking a real interest, spurred me on.

If you read my master's theses (available at thebiggestproblemintheworld.org), you'll see that my work builds upon and connects dots between the works of many others, and my work would not exist without theirs. I would like to thank them all, and Deanna Kuhn, Professor of Psychology and Education at Teachers College, Columbia University, in particular. I am also grateful, of course, to the participants in the 10 experiments I conducted in Cambridge and London, who, as promised, shall remain nameless.

Acknowledgments

Those who know me know of my love of libraries, and much of this work, including the writing of this handbook, has been done in one. I'd like to thank the staffs of The London Library; the British Library, London; the Cambridge University Library; the National Library of Scotland, Edinburgh; the Deichman Bjørvika, Oslo; the National Library of Norway, Oslo; the National Library of Sweden, Stockholm; and La Médiathèque – Ludothèque, Arcachon, for their help and providing me with comfortable places to work.

There are, of course, a lifetime of people to thank, from my "surrogate mother," Kathy Wolfe, at the Southwest Branch Library, where I worked in high school in Green Bay, Wisconsin, to my friend Steve Price, who sells *The Big Issue* on the Hungerford Bridge, Charing Cross, London, so my apologies to all of the people whose names do not appear in these Acknowledgments. In ways big and small, you, too, have had an impact on whom I've become and what appears on the pages of this handbook. I hope I've succeeded in letting each of you know of your importance to me.

1
The Myth of Problem Solving

We fail to solve solvable problems regularly.

Consider these headlines:

"More Bad News for a Fattening America"

"For Britain's Health Service, Little Cash but Big Demands"

"Income Distribution:
A Growing Gap Between Rich and Poor"

They read like today's news, but each is at least 20 years old. In other words, not one of these problems has been solved.

We have tried to solve some of them—at least we think we have. The health risks associated with obesity have been well publicized, for example, and nutritional information is widely available. Over the last 50 years, the diet and fitness industries have grown significantly, too, especially in the United States.

Yet over the last 45 years, the worldwide obesity rate has nearly tripled. In 2016, nearly three out of four adults in the US were overweight, and almost half, about three times the global average, weren't just overweight, but obese. Soon, the annual cost of obesity-related illnesses is estimated to exceed $1 trillion globally, to say nothing of the lives lost.

Solvable problems and progress

Sometimes problems are unsolvable because the knowledge we need to solve them hasn't been discovered. There may be a disease, for example, with no known cure.

The headlines above, however, refer to solvable problems. We know they are solvable because they have been solved before. Income inequality has improved in Britain since the 1800s. Health service funding is largely a matter of priorities. And as the World Health Organization reminds us, "Obesity is preventable," although while it is most of the time, it isn't always.

Only by solving problems do we progress. When any problem goes unsolved, we move sideways through life at best.

Unlike with unsolvable problems, we choose whether or not to solve solvable ones. When we choose not to solve them, we choose not to progress. Experiencing pain that was avoidable, we choose a lower quality of life and sometimes a shorter life instead.

If I am obese, for instance, and choose not to lose weight, I invite certain illnesses, like heart disease and strokes, and other risks and challenges, and I will suffer in ways I needn't have.

When I choose not to solve a personal problem, I will cause myself to suffer unnecessarily. When we choose not to solve societal problems, like income inequality, we will cause a number of people to suffer unnecessarily, sometimes including ourselves.

A matter of perspective?

"How far away is Robert Street?" the woman asked as we got on the bus in London. It was 9:35 on a weekday morning.

"About 20 minutes," the driver said.

"Really?" she mouthed to a passenger, who seemed to know and nodded.

The door closed, and the bus merged into heavy traffic.

The minutes ticked away, but the bus made little progress. Standing by the driver's side, the woman grew agitated—she didn't say a word, but she didn't have to.

Finally, "This traffic is terrible!" she said. "I am never going to make it to my interview on time."

"When is your interview?" a passenger asked.

"9:30," she said.

Getting on the bus at 9:35 for a 9:30 appointment, she wasn't late because of the traffic. That appointment probably wasn't the first the woman had missed, and until she solves her time-management problem, it won't be the last.

Problems are like truths. By definition, a truth remains true whether we believe it or not. The world has been warming recently whatever our beliefs.

Similarly, our problems remain ours whether or not we accept responsibility for them. And unless we're lucky, they will go unsolved until we solve them.

When we deny responsibility for our problems, we choose not to solve them. So, when our solvable problems go unsolved, are we denying responsibility for them? Or is something else going on, and if so, what?

Back to school

I suspected something else was going on—in general, we like progress and dislike suffering—but I wasn't sure what that something else could be.

In my search for an answer, I went back to school in 2012, this time for a master's in psychology and education at the University of Cambridge. I was 47 years old. I graduated with a distinction in 2015 and more questions than answers, so I continued my psychology studies in London.

I grew up in Manitowoc, Wisconsin, and not coming from money, I went to college in Texas on academic scholarships and grants. Then, after business school, I spent over two decades working, mainly in New York, rising through the corporate ranks. Eventually, I led a handful of organizations with people scattered around the world, so I traveled a lot too.

Wherever I went—Europe, North America, South America, Asia, Africa; from the Skeleton Coast of Namibia to Paris; from Almaty, Kazakhstan, to Buenos Aires—I saw people struggling to solve their problems. But I didn't have to leave home to see it. Friends, family members, colleagues and I struggled too.

If individuals struggle to solve their problems, it isn't surprising that the world struggles to solve so many: A society and its institutions, like its governments and businesses, are composed of those same people.

I finished my studies in 2019, but this time I had more answers.

The myth of problem solving

We depend on others to help us solve our problems, and it's our educators, namely our parents and teachers, that we depend on most. Many of us spend much of the first two decades of our lives in education, formally (at school) and informally (at home), presumably being prepared to solve life's problems.

At times, we depend on politicians, doctors, lawyers, executives, academics, consultants and others too. Either we have to, they have what's considered a good education, they're viewed as smart, or we think they have experience or expertise that will make them helpful. We pay for their services, work for them, vote for them and buy their books.

Their offerings seem endless, and they promise solutions to virtually every problem under the sun.

Despite the educations, intelligence, experience and expertise, however, many solvable problems go unsolved, regardless of the stakes. So, why?

Solving a problem is first and foremost dependent on our understanding of it.

2
Our Problem with Problems

Our understanding of problems is often incorrect.

Einstein once said that a problem's formulation (I explain what that means below) is often more important than its solution. Yet the formulation of a problem is *always* more important than its solution because you can't solve a problem without it.

Problems and their misrepresentation

Think of every problem that requires deliberate thought as if it were a story. Some problems, like deciding when and where to move if something is thrown at you, are solved unconsciously and quickly. Others, like deciding whether or not to continue your education, require consideration. Like a story, every one of these problems should have a beginning, middle and end.

The *beginning* is the situation you're in that's, well, problematic. Something is wrong, and you want to do something about it. Let's say that I'm overweight.

The *end* is your goal—it's where you'd rather be. Being overweight, I want to be a healthy weight.

The *middle* is a solution (there may be more than one), or a way to go from where you are to where you'd rather be. To lose weight, I can diet, exercise, both or more.

Together, each problem's beginning, middle and end are its *formulation*. It's our *representation*—think of it as a description or model—of the problem.

We *misrepresent* a problem when the beginning, middle or end is wrong or missing.

When we think of problems as stories, we can see that the woman on the bus in the last chapter is no stranger. At times, each of us has assumed a problem was one thing only to later understand or admit that it was another.

Each of us has also had goals only to later discover or accept that they should have been different. Or we've had no goal—we didn't like where we were, but we didn't know where we'd rather be.

And if the beginning or end is incorrect or missing, there can be no middle, or solution: You cannot go from a beginning to an end if there is no beginning or end, and you cannot solve your problem if one of them is wrong. Even knowing the beginning and end, we may not know how to solve our problem.

Whatever the case, unless luck intervenes, a misrepresented problem will continue, no matter how hard we work, how much time and money we spend, or how many tears we shed trying to solve it.

Take my own struggles with work. For the most part, my work life has been a pretty good one—I've had interesting jobs and worked with good people. Yet several years ago, I found myself becoming increasingly unhappy in my work.

Typically, unhappiness is a symptom rather than the problem itself, so if we want to be happy, we need to solve the problems causing our unhappiness. For years I struggled to figure out *why* I was unhappy (my beginning) and where I'd rather be (my end). Until those were clear, solving my problem was out of the question. Still, I tried different things—I changed companies and jobs and jobs within companies—but I was never lucky enough to stumble upon a solution.

Eventually, however, I realized that while I had looked many places for the cause of my unhappiness, I had neglected to look deeply enough within myself.

In his book *Escape from Freedom*, the psychologist Erich Fromm suggests that most people want what they *should* want in their educations, relationships, jobs, possessions and so on, according to their societies. They accept these cookie-cutter goals as their own because to figure out what one really wants is a difficult problem to solve, and they either don't know how or don't want to do the work required to solve it.

So, we give up parts of ourselves as we compromise and strive to become like others. In conforming, though, we can end up forsaking the best parts of ourselves, or those things that make each of us unique and our world a richer place. When we are not ourselves, so to speak, in the most important of ways for too long, unhappiness is inevitable. We have chosen not to solve the problem of becoming our own person.

I learned that there were important parts of myself, interests I had, that I had neglected for too long. Had I kept ignoring them, I would not have returned to school in my late 40s, and I would not have been able to write this handbook. Not coming from wealth, not having become independently wealthy and sacrificing income, I took real risks and incurred real costs to do those things, but therein lies real evidence of their value to me.

Every one of us has to decide whether we are going to be our own person or a puppet of sorts, others—our parents and the Establishment, for instance—pulling the strings. The problem is ours regardless, and unless we're lucky, it will go unsolved until we solve it.

Well-told stories and ill-defined problems

A good representation is a well-told story, and it must be two things: complete and accurate. With a good representation, problem solving becomes possible; without it, unless we're lucky, it does not.

Complete means that the story has a beginning, middle and end. *Accurate*, of course, means that each of those is essentially correct.

Unfortunately, virtually every problem in life is ill defined, meaning that the beginning, middle or end is somehow unclear. Sometimes they are important problems, such as deciding if you should marry (or leave) someone; sometimes they aren't, such as figuring out what to eat for dinner one night. Regardless, in their haziness, these problems, most problems, are susceptible to misrepresentation. Their stories are likely to be incomplete or inaccurate, so poorly told, and we will struggle to solve them until we better represent them.

Intelligence, education and ill-defined problems

We often assume that intelligent people are better than average at solving problems. While we're right with regard to certain well-defined problems, like the math and science problems found in schools and labs, those are not most problems.

When people talk about intelligence, they're usually referring to *cognitive intelligence*, or the math and language skills measured by IQ tests and needed to solve well-defined problems. Cognitive intelligence, however, plays little-to-no role in solving ill-defined problems. "Smart" people, it turns out, are no better than average at solving most problems and worse than we expect them to be.

Emotional intelligence, what's become a buzz phrase for someone's ability to identify and understand their emotions and others' as well as reason and solve problems with that understanding, has been suggested as being important to ill-defined problem solving too.

The concept of emotional intelligence was introduced to the general public in the mid-'90s, and great claims were made regarding its power. In 1995, for example, a *Time* cover stated that emotional intelligence may be success's best predictor and redefine smartness. Unfortunately, little emotional intelligence research had been conducted at the time, and no means of measuring it existed. In other words, those claims were baseless.

Today people commonly refer to emotional intelligence. They believe they know what it is and how to spot and evaluate it. But they are mistaken.

Since the mid-'90s, research has made clear that we do not know what emotional intelligence is. Needless to say, if we do not know what it is, we cannot measure it. And if we cannot measure emotional intelligence, we cannot determine its importance to problem solving or anything else.

Unfortunately, much of our world continues to overemphasize the importance of these intelligences, and with regard to cognitive intelligence, particularly in education. Research, however, suggests that no level of undergraduate education and perhaps no education past primary school matters to our ability to solve ill-defined problems.

Yet that finding isn't surprising: Education currently emphasizes the development of the math and language skills used to solve well-defined problems. In general, schools and universities aren't teaching us what matters to solving most of life's problems.

Most of us know people who were successful in school, but once they left it, they struggled, perhaps at work, in their relationships or as parents. We also know people who didn't do well academically but went on to thrive personally and professionally. Indeed, "smart" people fail to solve problems often enough to suggest something else matters.

In short, if our goal is to become better at solving most problems, we need to redefine what it means to be smart, then teach it.

Overconfidence and expertise

In our desires for ease and, ironically, the avoidance of pain, we may overestimate our understanding of a problem and misrepresent it.

Quick, inexpensive and simple solutions become attractive too. How often have you been tempted by someone to follow "just a few simple steps" to improve your relationship, find a job or just feel happier, for example? It's seductive, for sure. Yet when you've done so, how often has it not worked?

To some extent, the answer depends on whether the expertise upon which you've relied is genuine or self-proclaimed. To accurately represent a problem, we must determine what is relevant to it; if we include something irrelevant, we may misrepresent the problem. Genuine expertise affects whether and to what extent we focus on what's relevant. Real experts can help us solve problems; self-proclaimed "experts" muddle the picture.

Real expertise, however, also can undermine our problem-representation efforts. An expert's focus can cause them to ignore something relevant outside of their often-narrow view. While experts often think highly of one another, those views are often poor guides to their performance, so we should question experts too.

Our knowledge is limited, of course, and not being able to pick our problems, we will not be experts with regard to most of them. Often, we will depend on others to help us represent and solve our problems, so we need to know how to assess their expertise if we are to choose them wisely. Actors, models and reality TV "stars," for example, may be experts in their crafts, but that doesn't make them experts elsewhere. Chapter 3 will help you better identify those upon whom it is safe to rely.

When we approach our problems with overconfidence, we fail to acknowledge what we don't know, so we will not seek expertise when we should. If we're simply honest with ourselves about what we know, however, the problem of overconfidence is easily solved.

Our problem with problems

Our problems often go unsolved, regardless of the stakes, because despite our educations and intelligence, our representations are incomplete or inaccurate, and we don't know it. We think we're solving our problems, but we're not.

If we visualize what's happening, this oval represents these misrepresented problems and the focus of the effort, time, money and emotion we spend trying to solve them:

Lying outside of that oval, our goal, the dot, is not the focus of that spending, but we don't realize it. So, our problems continue. We gain weight. Income inequality worsens. I could go on, but I don't have to—you can see it yourself, daily.

What we need to do is spend our time, effort, money and emotion on solving problems for which we have well-told stories, or those that have complete and accurate representations:

The goal, the dot, is their focus. Luck aside, only problems with well-told stories are solvable.

3
Why Truth Matters

*We misrepresent our problems
more often than not.*

Growing up, we are often told to tell the truth, even if we rarely get a good explanation as to why. It's just considered "good" and "the right thing to do." Nevertheless, lying seems common. The cover of *Time* even asked, "Is Truth Dead?"

Why truth matters
The truth, however, will always matter because no problem can be solved until it has been accurately represented.

Falsehoods
Actually, lies are less common than we think—they just get more press. That's not to say that lies aren't a problem and sometimes a very big problem. It's just that most of the falsehoods we encounter in our lives are, unlike lies, unintentional and the result of negligence or honest mistakes.

Most lies, it turns out, are actually told by a relative few prolific liars. Unfortunately, sometimes they are in powerful positions. Yet usually liars lie to benefit themselves, and they are always shortsighted: Their inevitable failure to solve the problems they misrepresent eventually will expose them.

In June 2016, for example, the citizens of the United Kingdom voted to leave the European Union. In the run-up to this "Brexit" vote, in their attempt to woo voters, certain "leave" campaigners claimed that the costs saved by leaving would allow the government to generously fund the country's impoverished National Health Service.

The touted cost savings, however, were exaggerated. They ignored the value of benefits received from the EU, such as payments to UK farmers, and included rebates, money that the UK never paid and therefore could not be saved. In other words, the leave campaigners' claims were false, and they misrepresented the problem.

So, while the UK has left the EU, perhaps some "leave" votes having been won on pretense, the NHS problem remains for something other than Brexit to solve. Despite promises, Brexit will not solve any problem that has been misrepresented because it cannot.

The importance of arguing

I can't tell you what is true, but I can help you figure that out yourself. Only truths allow us to represent problems, then solve them, so the ability to arrive at and identify truths is invaluable. And you can possess it.

Truths are determined by sound arguments. Rather than between people, most of that arguing is done in our minds, silently, and it is how we think critically.

An *argument* is an iterative process of claims and counterclaims, each supported by evidence:

Two things determine whether an argument is sound:

1) the robustness of the process, meaning that there are enough claim-counterclaim iterations to move us toward or arrive at a truth, and
2) the soundness of the evidence, the successful defense of each claim and counterclaim being dependent upon it.

Let's say, for instance, someone claims that the relatively high number of shootings in the US is due to easy access to guns. A member of a gun rights group counters them by saying that easy access has nothing to do with it. That is an exchange, not a sound argument: There were no iterations, and neither person provided evidence, sound or otherwise.

Unfortunately, research shows that we argue poorly more often than not. Usually, we don't consider counterclaims or evidence—we fail to notice when they are missing and draw conclusions in their absence. When we do consider evidence, it is often unsound.

In other words, not having been taught how to think critically, we're not very good at getting to truths or identifying falsehoods. More often than not, we rely on untruths without realizing it and misrepresent our problems, so they continue.

Opinions and anecdotes

Without sound evidence to support them, claims and counterclaims are merely opinions. Anyone can have one, and most people do. In the gun control example mentioned, opinions were exchanged. And opinions do not lead to nor are they equivalent to truths.

Rather than truths and approximations of them, much, if not most of the world operates on opinions and anecdotes that we take for granted, and we operate poorly as a consequence.

When we rely on unsound evidence, often that means we'll take one example, an anecdote, and generalize from it to draw an incorrect conclusion. Let's say you read a book by a successful entrepreneur in which they share the "secrets" of their success. So, you get inspired—it sounds good, especially the "successful" part—and decide to follow their advice.

One person's success, however, is a function of many things: Sometimes it's due to qualities they possess, sometimes they're in the right place at the right time (they're lucky), often it's a function of both of those things and more. And many of those things aren't replicable—what worked for them probably isn't going to work for you. It's only by looking for replicable qualities shared by many successful entrepreneurs that you may find qualities worth emulating.

While it can be inspiring, another person's story is largely just that: someone else's story. It is never our own, regardless of how much we or they may want it to be.

Cause and effect: In evidence and making plans

Recently, I read about a teenager suffering from severe anxiety, a serious and growing problem amongst people in general. When asked about failing a quiz in high school, the young man concluded that he'd get a bad grade in the class, wouldn't get into the university he wanted, wouldn't get a good job, and that he would be "a total failure." All of that from failing a single quiz.

I couldn't help but think how a better understanding of cause and effect, or causality, and correlation would help him and so many others to worry and suffer less. *Correlation* refers to the extent to which two things coexist. Think of *causation* as a special form of correlation in which two things don't just coexist, but one of the two things causes the other to happen.

An understanding of causation and correlation is important to problem representation, too, because you can't tell a problem's story without it.

Firstly, evidence's soundness—and therefore truth—is dependent on it. With regard to our arguments and their claims and counterclaims, causal evidence is of greater value than correlational evidence, and when evidence is neither of those two things, it's of no value.

Secondly, it usually takes several steps to solve problems, particularly difficult ones. So, we need to make plans, and only an understanding of causation and correlation enables us to do so. If my goal is to lose weight, for example, then I need to know *how* diet and exercise can impact someone's weight and consider those things and more to make a plan to lose it.

Let's say, for instance, that ten people are on a specific diet, and each of them loses weight. Now, are the diet and weight loss correlated? Is the diet causing the weight loss? Many, perhaps most people would say they are correlated, and the diet works because ten people were on it, and they all lost weight. The correct answer, though, is we can't tell.

To claim the diet and weight loss correlate, we also need to look at ten people who did *not* go on the diet. If all of those people lost weight, we can't claim the diet and weight loss correlate because an equal number of people who *weren't* on the diet lost weight too. If none of those people lost weight, however, it is relatively safe to assume that the diet and weight loss correlate highly. And if only some of those people lost weight, the diet and weight loss correlate to some extent.

Causation is much harder to prove. Even if the weight loss and diet are correlated, I can't say the diet caused the weight loss unless I have proven that every other factor that could have caused it didn't. By doing that, I prove that the diet is the sole cause of the weight loss, but that is a very difficult, often impractical, if not impossible, thing to do.

Our world, a world of ill-defined problems, is an imperfect one in which we rarely have control over all of those other factors—often we don't even know what they are—so most of the time correlation is as good as it gets. The stronger the underlying correlation, the greater the comfort you can take in relying on the evidence in your arguments.

If we go back to the teen's anxiety, with proper education it should be easy for him and others to see that failing one quiz does not cause someone to get a bad grade in a class. And getting one bad grade in a class does not cause someone to fail to get into their university of choice and so on. And none of those things leads to becoming "a total failure."

For most of us, an understanding of causation and correlation is possible. Yet in general, adults have difficulty identifying and distinguishing between causal and correlational relationships regardless of undergraduate education. They readily misinterpret correlational relationships or no relationship at all as causal in nature.

On most days I get a coffee after lunch at the same place in London. One day the guy who usually makes my coffee said he'd eaten so much pizza lately that he was worried he might turn into a pizza. Just as someone who fails one quiz will not become a total failure for having failed it, my coffee guy doesn't have to worry.

4
The Biggest Problem in the World

Once we solve our problem with problems,
we can solve other problems.

Eldridge Cleaver, an American political activist in the '60s and '70s, once said if you are not part of the solution, you are part of the problem, and it is a truth: You cannot be both.

Let's say shootings are a problem in my country due in part to lax regulation. If I am a politician with the power to pass stricter gun laws, I have to choose whether I will support those laws or not. If I choose not to support them, shootings may occur that could have been avoided, and I will be partly responsible for them. If I am not that politician, but I have the right to vote, and I choose not to vote for a candidate who supports those laws, then I will be partly responsible for those shootings too.

If you are not part of the solution, you are part of the problem.

The biggest problem in the world

No problem can be solved until it has been completely and truthfully represented. Yet virtually every one of us argues poorly—from our political and business leaders to our friends, colleagues, relatives and ourselves. Failing to think critically, we end up relying on untruths without realizing it and misrepresenting our problems more often than not. Until we become better at representing our problems, or solving our problem with problems, we will fail to solve our other problems regularly.

Luck

In 2016, Steven Levitt, an economics professor at the University of Chicago and co-author of the book *Freakonomics*, wrote a paper entitled "Heads or Tails: The Impact of a Coin Toss on Major Life Decisions and Subsequent Happiness." In it, he suggests that we would be better off tossing a coin and relying on luck to solve the most important problems in our lives rather than thinking through them.

Imagine flipping a coin to decide if you should marry (or divorce) someone, have a baby, further your education, take (or quit) a job, lose weight or vote.

But this research illustrates my point: When we tell the wrong stories, we can expect to solve our problems no more often than if by chance. Let's go back to the oval:

Our goal, the dot, is not the focus of the effort, time, money and emotion we spend trying to solve a misrepresented problem. So, whenever we try to solve a misrepresented problem, only luck will get us to our goal.

Chance is the last thing you want to depend on when it comes to solving the most important problems in your life because it is unreliable. And heartless—it does not care if you suffer or die. Relying on chance becomes attractive only when you have no alternative. Yet without realizing it, because we misrepresent our problems more often than not, we're relying on luck to solve our problems regularly.

Squandering

Two centuries ago, Joseph de Maistre, a French lawyer, said (in French, of course), "Every nation has the government it deserves." Sometimes this is misinterpreted as people get the politicians they deserve. When people vote for politicians who fail them, however, do they "deserve" them? It is naïve and arrogant to think so.

It is not surprising that people often vote for politicians who fail them: The problem of voting wisely gets misrepresented too. When we don't vote wisely, our votes are wasted as is the hard-won right to cast them.

When we misrepresent any problem, the time, money, effort and emotion we spend trying to solve it is wasted. And because we misrepresent problems so often, we waste an awful lot of all of those things.

When it comes to education, for instance, only one country in the Organization for Economic Cooperation and Development (OECD), a group of so-called developed countries, spent more than the US's $18,000 per student in 2017. That's about 60% more than the OECD average of $11,200. If you exclude the amounts spent on post-secondary education and peripheral services, such as research and development, the US spent about $12,400 per student, or about 30% more than the OECD average of $9,500.

Yet in the 2015 Programme for International Student Assessment (PISA), a respected test used to evaluate education, US 15-year-olds achieved only average scores on science and reading and below-average scores on math.

Average spending for average scores is expected; above-average spending for average and below-average scores is wasteful. Assuming there are about 56 million students in US preschools, elementary schools and secondary schools in 2020, the US spends over \$160 billion a year on education that, according to PISA, has no benefit. If higher education and peripheral services are included, there are about 76 million students in the US in 2020, and the US spends over \$500 billion a year for education with no benefit.

But that's an understatement, and the US is not alone in its wastefulness. Remember, education is not currently focused on teaching the skills necessary to solve most of life's problems, and PISA doesn't measure them. In other words, much of the \$9,500-11,200 that's spent on average annually educating each OECD student worldwide is wasted too.

Needless to say, what we waste trying to solve misrepresented problems is not available for solving those we can. The money misspent on education; the \$1 trillion or so spent annually treating largely preventable obesity-related illnesses; the money misspent on healthcare in the US to achieve, like in education, sub-par results; and much, much more—wasted, as is the accompanying time, effort and emotion.

What we could achieve if it were invested wisely! And we could stop borrowing and taxing unnecessarily to do it. We could solve problems and progress rather than go nowhere or backwards.

Becoming part of the solution

Over 50 years ago, Daniel P. Moynihan, a former US Senator, wrote an article for *The New York Times*: "To Solve a Problem, One Must First Define It." Although the article highlighted the importance of problem representation, it failed to identify our problem with it, our problem with problems.

Focusing on ill-fated solutions rather than the representations upon which they are dependent, we have overlooked our problem with problems for a long time, and we have paid a heavy price. We have wasted too much, achieved too little and suffered unnecessarily.

Like the problems of income inequality, obesity and so many others, our problem with problems is solvable too. Unlike those problems, however, we haven't known we've had it. Until now.

In not teaching us to think critically nor preparing us to solve most of life's problems, our educations have failed us, and as with poor politicians, we haven't deserved it. When one out of three American adults has an undergraduate degree, but fewer than one out of 50 reads at a college level, we know something is amiss in education. When earnings potential tells us that possession of an undergraduate degree is more valuable than the education underlying it, we know something is amiss in society too.

Too often we are seduced by and settle for the superficial. We strive for educations but neglect to consider what's being taught. We obsess over polls, wanting to know what people think, yet overlook understanding why they think it (which may explain why pollsters often get it wrong). And we are sometimes desperate for solutions to our problems, but often fail to first understand the problems themselves.

Education is a means, not an end, and learning how to solve most of life's problems should be its primary purpose.

So, for now, in the absence of that education, how can you better represent your problems and evaluate the representations of others?

- Know a problem's beginning, middle and end (BME).
- Make sure the BME is essentially correct, or true.

To know the BME and ensure that truthfulness:

- Be honest with yourself about what you know.
- When you don't know something, find a real expert, but question them too.
- Seek new perspectives, not just the familiar.

- Rely on sound arguments, evidence included, and disregard individual opinions and anecdotes.
- Ensure sufficient correlation or causation underlies your evidence and plans.

Solving our problem with problems doesn't mean that we will solve our other problems—things like fear, laziness and impatience can still get in the way—but it makes solution possible.

To be part of the solution is to choose to tell a complete story and a truthful one. Our problem with problems is ours regardless, and it will go unsolved until we solve it.

If we choose not to solve our problem with problems, our problems will continue. Obesity rates will rise. Income inequality will worsen. We will continue to vote for politicians who fail us. And unsolved problems often lead to others, so instead of fewer problems, we may have more.

To solve problems is to progress, and to progress is to live. How well we live is determined by the problems we solve. The goal is not a problem-free, suffering-free existence: As long as we want to progress, there will be problems to solve. The goal is to become better at solving them, so we welcome rather than run from them, confident in our ability to overcome them. We will know that any suffering will be necessary. And we will know that we have truly lived.

In writing this book, I wish for your best possible life, and I hope you will now want to solve the problems necessary to achieve it.

For more information or to contact the author, please visit www.thebiggestproblemintheworld.org.

Principal Sources

This handbook is primarily dependent on my two unpublished master's theses, including their 10 underlying experiments, available at thebiggestproblemintheworld.org:

Balzan, R. (2014). *Now with feeling: The impact of "emotional intelligence" on everyday problem solving.* University of Cambridge.

Balzan, R. (2019). *Our problem with problems: Problem representations (and why truth matters).* University of London.

Chapter 1

Centers for Disease Control and Prevention, National Center for Health Statistics. (2018). *Obesity and overweight.* https://www.cdc.gov/nchs/fastats/obesity-overweight.htm

Deaton, A., & Case, A. (2020). *Deaths of despair and the future of capitalism.* Princeton University Press.

Grady, D. (2000, August 27). More bad news for a fattening America. *The New York Times.*

Levy, F. (1988, May 1). Income distribution: A growing gap between rich and poor. *The New York Times.*

Lohr, S. (1988, August 7). For Britain's Health Service, little cash but big demands. *The New York Times.*

World Health Organization. (2020). *Obesity and overweight.* https://www.who.int/news-room/fact-sheets/detail/obesity-and-overweight

World Obesity Federation. (2017). *Calculating the costs of the consequences of obesity.* https://www.worldobesity.org/resources/resource-library/calculating-the-costs-of-the-consequences-of-obesity

Chapter 2

Burgman, M. A., McBride, M., Ashton, R., Speirs-Bridge, A., Flander, L., Wintle, B., ... Twardy, C. (2011). Expert status and performance. *PLOS ONE, 6*(7), e22998.

Chase, W., & Simon, H. (1973). Perception in chess. *Cognitive Psychology, 4*(1), 55–81.

Einstein, A., & Infeld, L. (1938). *The evolution of physics: The growth of ideas from early concepts to relativity and quanta.* Cambridge University Press.

Fromm, E. (1941). *Escape from freedom.* Holt, Rinehart and Winston.

Galotti, K. (1989). Approaches to studying formal and everyday reasoning. *Psychological Bulletin, 105*(3), 331–351.

Gardner, H. (1983). *Frames of mind: The theory of multiple intelligences.* Basic Books.

Hayes, J., & Simon, H. (1977). Psychological differences among problem isomorphs. In N. Castellan, D. Pisoni, & G. Potts (Eds.), *Cognitive theory* (Vol. 2, pp. 21–41). Erlbaum.

Kahneman, D. (2011). *Thinking, fast and slow.* Farrar, Straus and Giroux.

Kahneman, D., & Klein, G. (2009). Conditions for intuitive expertise: A failure to disagree. *American Psychologist, 64*(6), 515–526.

Ottati, V., Price, E., Wilson, C., & Sumaktoyo, N. (2015). When self-perceptions of expertise increase closed-minded cognition: The earned dogmatism effect. *Journal of Experimental Social Psychology, 61*, 131–138.

Perkins, D. (1985). Postprimary education has little impact on informal reasoning. *Journal of Educational Psychology*, *77*(5), 562–571.

Reitman, W. (1965). *Cognition and thought: An information-processing approach*. Wiley.

Salovey, P., & Mayer, J. (1990). Emotional intelligence. *Imagination, Cognition and Personality*, *9*(3), 185–211.

Sternberg, R., Wagner, R., Williams, W., & Horvath, J. (1995). Testing common sense. *American Psychologist*, *50*(11), 912–927.

Time. (1995, October 2). *Time*, *146*(14).

Wigdor, A., & Garner, W. (Eds.). (1982). *Ability testing: Uses, consequences, and controversies. Part 1: Report of the Committee*. National Academy Press.

Chapter 3

Agosta, S., Pezzoli, P., & Sartori, G. (2013). How to detect deception in everyday life and the reasons underlying it. *Applied Cognitive Psychology*, *27*(2), 256–262.

Billig, M. (1987). *Arguing and thinking: A rhetorical approach to social psychology*. Cambridge University Press.

Bond, J., & DePaulo, B. (2006). Accuracy of deception judgments. *Personality and Social Psychology Review*, *10*(3), 214–234.

Denizet-Lewis, B. (2017, October 11). Why are more American teenagers than ever suffering from severe anxiety? *The New York Times*.

DePaulo, B., Kirkendol, S., Kashy, D., Wyer, M., & Epstein, J. (1996). Lying in everyday life. *Journal of Personality and Social Psychology*, *70*(5), 979–995.

Full Fact. (2017). *£350 million EU claim "a clear misuse of official statistics"*. https://fullfact.org/europe/350-million-week-boris-johnson-statistics-authority-misuse/

Halevy, R., Shalvi, S., & Verschuere, B. (2014). Being honest about dishonesty: Correlating self-reports and actual lying. *Human Communication Research, 40*(1), 54–72.

Kuhn, D. (1991). *The skills of argument.* Cambridge University Press.

Kuhn, D., Phelps, E., & Walters, J. (1985). Correlational reasoning in an everyday context. *Journal of Applied Developmental Psychology, 6,* 85–97.

Levine, T., Park, H., & McCornack, S. (1999). Accuracy in detecting truths and lies: Documenting the "veracity effect." *Communication Monographs, 66*(2), 125–144.

Serota, K., & Levine, T. (2015). A few prolific liars: Variation in the prevalence of lying. *Journal of Language and Social Psychology, 34*(2), 138–157.

Serota, K., Levine, T., & Boster, F. (2010). The prevalence of lying in America: Three studies of self-reported lies. *Human Communication Research, 36*(1), 2–25.

Time. (2017, April 3). *Time, 189*(12).

Toulmin, S. (1958). *The uses of argument.* Cambridge University Press.

Chapter 4

Institute of Education Sciences, National Center for Education Statistics. (2020). *Fast facts: Back to school statistics.* https://nces.ed.gov/fastfacts/display.asp?id=372

Levitt, S. (2016). *Heads or tails: The impact of a coin toss on major life decisions and subsequent happiness* (Working Paper No. 22487). National Bureau of Economic Research.

Maistre, J. de (1851). *Lettres et opuscules inédits du Comte J. de Maistre: Précédés d'une notice biographique* (Vol. 1). Vaton.

Moynihan, D. (1970, January 12). To solve a problem, one must first define it. *The New York Times.*

Organization for Economic Cooperation and Development. (2016). *Skills matter: Further results from the survey of adult skills.* https://www.oecd-ilibrary.org/education/skills-matter_9789264258051-en

Organization for Economic Cooperation and Development. (2018). *PISA 2015 results in focus.* https://www.oecd.org/pisa/pisa-2015-results-in-focus.pdf

Organization for Economic Cooperation and Development. (2020). *Education at a glance 2020: OECD indicators. Indicator C1. How much is spent per student on educational institutions?* https://www.oecd-ilibrary.org/education/education-at-a-glance-2020_69096873-en

United States Census Bureau. (2017). *Highest educational levels reached by adults in the U.S. since 1940* [press release]. https://www.census.gov/newsroom/press-releases/2017/cb17-51.html

Lightning Source UK Ltd.
Milton Keynes UK
UKHW021839071121
393549UK00006B/1080